ARTHUR MILLER

DRAMATISTS
PLAY SERVICE
INC.

ELEGY FOR A LADY
Copyright © 1982, Arthur Miller
Copyright © 1980, Arthur Miller

All Rights Reserved

PLAYWRIGHT'S NOTE

It never before occurred to me to add a note of explanation to a play in published form. A playwright expects to be misinterpreted to some important degree, but to confront total incomprehension on the part of the critics is a new experience. This is especially strange when among the public there were more than enough people who expressed a perfectly adequate understanding and appreciation of what they had seen. In the hope that the interested audience and readers of this play not be permanently misled I would make certain fundamental observations.

The play is The Man's revery. It is not a dream but the kind of waking projection the mind often ventures into when it is stymied by life. Through this revery he makes it possible to confront if not the dying woman he loves then his fears about the truth of their relationship.

The actor must understand that there are bad implications for his character, and worse yet for hers in this confrontation. The relationship may turn out not to have had any meaning at all, something that would threaten his own reality. But however he may be judged, The Man cannot bear to accept living without the truth whatever it may cost his self-esteem.

The setting should combine a certain super emphasis on dream elements, like the mannikin parts scattered everywhere, and at the same time elements that are real and substantial and logical. Again, this is not a dream; The Man is awake and aware. Actually, he has been searching through stores for something that will signify his inexpressibly contradictory feelings for his beloved. In the end, the "perfection" which The Proprietress discovers is simply the completion, the fullest flowering of their relationship within its given limits, namely, both their natures, his age, the society and the life he has lived. He cannot, in short, have everything and he tastes acceptance of reality, the filling of bounds, a sense of form.

The Proprietress, as he envisions her, is packing up the store's contents from the beginning of the play until the shelves are empty and nothing is left but the bare structure of the set, the occasion of his vision.

The play, being his revery, is basically his viewpoint; thus The Proprietress must be played with the feelings of a woman who loves him but who understands the condition of their relationship. At the same time, however, he is not dreaming and he insists on her having her own autonomy, her determination to deny the imminence of death; he also, in effect, insists on her contradicting him when he knows that she would, in life. He is in control of this vision but striving to stretch himself to embrace the unpalatable truth and even an ultimate dilemma, if that should turn out to be the case.

Primary to the role of The Man is the impact of his desperation; half-convinced he will never see his lover alive again he is racing time to find out what they meant to each other. It is painful to him that she might die without his having named their relation; he is thirsting for meaning, objectification, he wants to *see.*

Ideally, the part should be played with a doubled vision; he knows that in the literal sense The Proprietress is not his lover; he knows he has created this persona. But at the same time she has the same force for him as his lover. It is simply that within this revery he has the liberty to speak fully, to hurt himself and her, to fill their customarily observed gaps—as he would find it impossible to do in real life—in the hope of achieving a vision of them both in their real connection with one another. Because of her duality in his imagination, being both his lover and an abstract of her, she takes on another dimension of Womankind. But she must not be played "abstractly." She may weep and make her demands even more fully than she might have in life.

It may be asked, why this form, this enigma? The answer is simply that in revery he creates an arena in which to be free to say everything, an area of the imagination where he has the liberty to confront what he suspects she may be feeling in real life. It is also the place—perhaps its primary function for him is this—where he may glimpse the nothingness which is hounding him behind his back, as it were, in the hope of being victorious over it.

Finally, death being so near to both of them they are, needless to say, beyond any sentimentality. This tone may be difficult to grasp, however, in a theatre where all but insouciant irony and romance are feelings outlawed; but the integrative vision, the sense of putting things together, is a powerful feeling which the actor, perhaps unstylishly at present, is entitled to feel.

ELEGY FOR A LADY, in tandem with SOME KIND OF
LOVE STORY, was presented by the Long Wharf Theater
in New Haven, Connecticut, in November 1982 under
the omnibus title of 2 BY A.M. The production was
directed by the author, with Christine Lahti and Charles
Cioffi appearing in both plays. The sets were by Hugh
Landwehr; the costumes were by Bill Walker; and the
lighting was by Ronald Wallace.

Note: SOME KIND OF LOVE STORY is published by
Dramatists Play Service in a separate edition.

CAST

MAN
PROPRIETRESS

ELEGY FOR A LADY

The Man appears in a single beam of light, facing the audience. He is hatless, dressed in a well-fitted overcoat and tweed suit.

He stares as though lost in thought, slightly bent forward, perhaps to concentrate better. He is deep into himself, unaware for the moment of his surroundings.

Light rises behind him, gradually dawning across the stage, reveals aspects of what slowly turns out to be a boutique. The shop consists of its elements without the walls, the fragments seeming to be suspended in space.

A sweater is draped over a bust, a necklace on another bust, a garter on an upturned plastic thigh, a watch on an upturned arm, a knitted cap and muffler on a plastic head. Some of these stand on elements of the counter-shape, others seem to hang in air.

As the light rises to normal level the Man moves into the boutique. And now, among the displays a Woman is discovered standing motionless, looking off at an angle in passive thought. She is wearing a white silk blouse and a light beige skirt and high heeled shoes. The Man moves from object to object and pauses also to look into the display case in the counter where jewelry is kept. As he nears her, he halts, staring into her profile.

5

MAN. Can you help me?

PROPRIETRESS. (*Turns now to look into his eyes.*) Yes?

MAN. Do you have anything for a dying woman?

PROPRIETRESS. (*She waits a moment for him to continue and then looks about, trying to imagine.*) Well, let me see... (*He waits another instant, then resumes his search, examining a pair of gloves, a blouse.*) May I ask you if...? (*She breaks off when he does not respond or turn to her. Finally he does.*)

MAN. Excuse me?

PROPRIETRESS. I was just wondering if you meant that she was actually...

MAN. By the end of the month or so. Apparently.

PROPRIETRESS. (*Seeking hope.*) ...But it isn't sure.

MAN. I think *she's* sure. But I haven't talked to any doctors or anything like that...

PROPRIETRESS. And it's..?

MAN. (*Cutting in.*) So it seems, yes.

PROPRIETRESS. (*With helpless personal involvement.*) Ah.

MAN. (*Forcing out the words.*) ...I assume you were going to say cancer.

PROPRIETRESS. (*She nods with a slight inhale of air. Now she glances around at her stock with a new sense of urgency.*)

MAN. I started to send flowers, but flowers seem so...funereal.

PROPRIETRESS. Not necessarily. Some spring flowers?

MAN. What's a spring flower?—daisies?

PROPRIETRESS. Or daffodils. There's a shop two blocks down—Faynton's.

MAN. (*Considers.*) I passed there twice. But I couldn't decide if it should be a bunch of flowers or a plant.

PROPRIETRESS. Well, either would be...

MAN. Except that a bunch would fade, wouldn't they?—in a few days?

PROPRIETRESS. But a plant would last. For years, sometimes.

MAN. But there's a suggestion of irony in that. Isn't there?

PROPRIETRESS. (*Thinks.*) Cut flowers, then.

MAN. They don't last at all, though, and she'd have to watch them withering away every morning...

PROPRIETRESS. Yes. (*Slight pause. He resumes looking at*

things, handles a bracelet . . . half asking . . .) She is not an older woman.

MAN. She just turned thirty . . . a couple of months ago.

PROPRIETRESS. *(Inhales sharply.)*

MAN. I've never really bought her anything. It struck me this afternoon. Nothing at all.

PROPRIETRESS. *(Delicately.)* You've known each other very . . .

MAN. *(Grieving.)* That's always hard to remember exactly. I can never figure out whether we met two winters ago or three. *(A little laugh which she joins.)*—She never can either . . . but we've never been able to stay on the subject long enough . . . in fact, on any subject—Except one. *(Proprietress laughs softly and he joins her for an instant.)* I'm married.

PROPRIETRESS. *(Nods.)* Yes.

MAN. And a lot older, of course.

PROPRIETRESS. Oh, Well that's not always a . . . *(Does not finish.)*

MAN. . . . No, but it is in most cases. *(He glances around again.)* I tried to think of a book. But after all the reading I've done nothing occurs to me.

PROPRIETRESS. She is not religious.

MAN. No—Although we never talked about religion. I don't know whether to try to concentrate her mind or distract it. Everything I can think to send her seems ironical; every book seems either too sad or too comical; I can't think of anything that won't increase the pain of it.

PROPRIETRESS. Perhaps you're being too tender. Nothing you could send would be as terrible as what she knows. *(He considers this, nods slightly.)* People do make a kind of peace with it.

MAN. No; I think in her case the alarm never stops ringing; living is all she ever thought about.—She won't answer the phone anymore. She doesn't return my calls for days, a week sometimes. I think, well, maybe she wants me—you know—to disappear, but then she does call back and always makes an excuse for not having called earlier. And she seems so desperate for me to believe her that I forget my resentment and I try to offer to help again and she backs away again . . . and I end up not seeing her for weeks again. *(Slight pause.)* I even wonder some-

7

times if she's simply trying to tell me there's somebody else. I can't figure out her signal.

PROPRIETRESS. Yes. But then again it might simply be that she...

MAN. That's right...

PROPRIETRESS. ...Finds it unbearable to be cheated of someone she loves...

MAN. I'm so glad to hear you say that!—it's possible...(*With relief, deeper intimacy.*) Sometimes, you know, we're on the phone and suddenly she excuses herself—and there's silence for a whole minute or two. And then she comes back on with a fresh and forward-looking attitude and her voice clear. But a couple of times she's cut out a split second too late, and I hear the rush of sobbing before she can clap her hand to the receiver. And it just burns my mind—and then when she comes back on so optimistically I'm in a terrible conflict; should I insist on talking about the reality, or should I pretend to sort of swim along beside her?

PROPRIETRESS. She's in a hospital.

MAN. Not yet.—Although, frankly, I'm not really sure. She's never home anymore, I know that. Unless she's stopped answering her phone altogether.—Even before this happened she would do that; but she's on the phone practically all day in her work so its understandable. Not that I'm ruling out that she might have been staying elsewhere occasionally.—But of course I've no right to make any demands on her. Or even ask any questions. —What does this sound like to you?

PROPRIETRESS. It sounds like you'd simply like to thank her.

MAN. (*With a slight surprise.*) Say! That's exactly right, yes! ...I'd simply like to thank her. I'm so glad it sounds that way.

PROPRIETRESS. Well...why not just *do* that?

MAN. (*Anguished.*) But how can I without implying that she's coming to the end....? (*Breaks off.*)

PROPRIETRESS. But she's *said* she's...?

MAN. Not really in so many words; she just...as I told you ...breaks up on the phone or...

PROPRIETRESS. (*With anguish now.*) Then why are you so sure she's...?

8

MAN. Because they're evidently operating on her in about ten days. And she won't tell me which hospital.

PROPRIETRESS. ... When you say "evidently" ...

MAN. Well, I know she's had this growth, and there was pain for awhile—about last summer—but then it passed and she was told it was almost certainly benign. But ... (*He goes silent; stares at Proprietress.*) Amazing.

PROPRIETRESS. Yes?

MAN. I've never mentioned her at all to anyone. And she has never let on about me. I know that ... and we have close mutual friends who have no idea. And here I walk in and tell you everything, as though ... (*From an engaging chuckle the breath seems to suddenly go out of him and he sits weakly on a stool, struggling against helplessness.*)

PROPRIETRESS. Yes? (*He makes an attempt to resume looking around the store but it fails.*) When you passed here earlier today ...

MAN. (*With great relief.*) Yes, that's right, I remember that! You saw me then ...

PROPRIETRESS. You stared at the window for a very long time.

MAN. I was trying to think of something for her.

PROPRIETRESS. Yes, I could see you imagining; it moved me deeply—for her sake.

MAN. It's amazing how absolutely nothing is right. I've been all over this part of town. But every single thing makes some kind of statement that is simply ... not right.

PROPRIETRESS. I'm sure you're going to think of something.

MAN. I hope so!

PROPRIETRESS. Oh I'm sure!

MAN. It's partly, I think, that I don't know what I want to say because I'm not sure what I have a right to say—I mean someone my age ought to be past these feelings.—(*With sudden revulsion.*) I go on as though there's all the time in the world ...! (*He stands, quickened, looking at the goods again.*) That kerchief is beautiful.

PROPRIETRESS. It's silk. Paris. (*She unfurls it for him.*)

MAN. Lovely. How would you wear it?

PROPRIETRESS. Any way. Like this.. (*She drapes it over her shoulders.*)

MAN. Hm.

PROPRIETRESS. Or even as a bandanna. (She wraps it over *her hair.*)

MAN. But she wouldn't do that indoors.

PROPRIETRESS. Well ... she *could.*

MAN. No. I'm afraid it could taunt her.

PROPRIETRESS. (*Putting it back on her shoulders.*) Well, then —in bed, like this.

MAN. (*Tempted.*) It is the right shade.—You have her coloring, you know;—I can't get over it, walking in off the street like this and blabbing away.

PROPRIETRESS. A thing like that builds up: you never know who you'll suddenly be telling it to.

MAN. Except that you have a look in your eye.

PROPRIETRESS. (*Smiling.*) What kind of look?

MAN. (*Returns her smile.*) You're seeing me. (*Of the scarf, definitely now.*) That isn't right. (*She slips it off. He moves, looking about.*) ... I think it's also that you're just about her age.

PROPRIETRESS. Why would that matter?

MAN. Someone older usually forgets what thirty was really like.

PROPRIETRESS. But you remember?

MAN. I didn't used to—thirty is far back down the road for me; but when I'm with her it all flows back at the touch of her skin. I feel like a Hindu recalling a former life.

PROPRIETRESS. And what is thirty like?

MAN. Thirty is an emergency. Thirty is the top of the ridge from where you can see down both sides—the sun and the shadow, your youth and your dying in the same glance. It's the last year to believe that your life can radically change anymore. And now she's caught on that ridge, unable to move.—God... (*A surge of anguish.*) ... how *pleased* with herself she'd gotten lately!—her ambitions and plans really working out ... (*With a half-proud, half embarrassed grin.*) although tough too—she can snap your head back with a harsh truth, sometimes. But I don't mind, because all it is is her wide-open desire to live

10

and win. (He glances around at the objects.) So it's hard to think of something that won't suggest the end of all that...and those eyes closing.

PROPRIETRESS. I have a kind of warm negligee. That one up there.

MAN. (Looks up, studies it for a moment.) But that might look to her like something after you've had a baby.

PROPRIETRESS. Not necessarily.

MAN. Yes. Like when they stroll around the hospital corridors afterward...If she's very sick she'd have to be in a hospital gown, wouldn't she?

PROPRIETRESS. (Sharply, like a personal rebellion.) But everybody doesn't die of it! Not every case!

MAN. (Explosively.) But she weeps on the phone! I heard it!

PROPRIETRESS. (A personal outcry.) Well the thought of disfigurement is terrible, isn't it? (She turns away, pressing her abdomen. Pause.) You ought to write, and simply thank her.

MAN. (Asking...) But that has to sound like a goodbye!

PROPRIETRESS. You sound as though you never had a single intimate talk!

MAN. Oh yes, but not about...negative things, somehow.

PROPRIETRESS. You met only for pleasure.

MAN. Yes. But it was also that we both knew there was nowhere it could go. Not at my age. So things tend to float pretty much on the surface...

PROPRIETRESS. (Smiling.) Still, the point does come...

MAN. Surprisingly, yes...

PROPRIETRESS. When it begins to be an effort to keep it un-committed...

MAN. Yes, there's a kind of contradiction...

PROPRIETRESS. —To care and simultaneously not-care...

MAN. You can't find a breakthrough—it's like a fish falling in love with the sun; once he breaks water he can't breathe!—So maybe the whole thing really doesn't amount to anything very much. (Pause.)

PROPRIETRESS. (She re-folds a sweater he had opened up.) But you don't always look like this, do you?

MAN. How?

PROPRIETRESS. In pain.

MAN. I guess I'm still unable to understand what she means to me.—I've never felt this way about a death. Even my mother's and father's ... there has always been some unwelcome, tiny feeling of release; an obligation removed. But in her case, I feel I'm being pulled under myself and suffocated. (*Proprietress takes a deeper breath of air and runs a hand down her neck.*) What else do you have that might ...? (*He halts as he starts once again to look around at the merchandise.*) ... Wait! I know —a bed jacket! That's the kind of neutral—healthy people wear them too!

PROPRIETRESS. I haven't any.

MAN. Nothing at all?

PROPRIETRESS. You might try the department stores.

MAN. (*Greatly relieved.*) I will. I think that's what I want. A bed jacket doesn't necessarily *say* anything, you see?

PROPRIETRESS. That's true, there is something non-commital about a bed jacket. Try Saks.

MAN. Yes. Thanks very much.—I never dreamed I'd have such a conversation! (*Starts to button up. With embarrassment ...*) It really amazes me ... coming in here like this ...

PROPRIETRESS. I have an electric kettle if you'd care for a cup of tea.

MAN. ... Thanks, I wouldn't mind, thanks very much ... I simply can't get over it, ... I had no idea all this was in me. (*She goes behind the counter, throws a switch; he sits at the counter again.*) Are you the owner here? (*He opens his coat again.*)

PROPRIETRESS. (*Nods affirmatively, then ...*) You know, it may be a case of a woman who's simply terrified of an operation, that's all.—I'm that way.

MAN. (*Thinks, trying to visualize—then ...*) No, I think it would take a lot more to panic her like this. She's not an hysterical person, except once a month for a few hours, maybe.

PROPRIETRESS. She tends to objectify her situation.

MAN. That's it.

PROPRIETRESS. Sees herself.

MAN. Yes.

PROPRIETRESS. From a distance.

MAN. Yes, she has guts; really cool nerve right up to the moment she flies to pieces.

PROPRIETRESS. She's had to control because she's alone.

MAN. Yes; so something like this must be like opening a shower curtain and a wild animal jumps out.

PROPRIETRESS. She was never married.

MAN. Never. (*Begins to stare off and smile.*)

PROPRIETRESS. Something about her couldn't be.—Unless to you?

MAN. (*Joyfully.*) She has a marvellous, throaty, almost vulgar laugh; it can bend her forward and she even slaps her thigh like a hick comedian... (*Proprietress begins laughing.*) and gets so helpless she hangs on my arm and nearly pulls me down to the sidewalk. (*Proprietress laughs more deeply.*) One time at one of those very tiny cafe tables we both exploded laughing at the same instant, and our heads shot forward just as the waiter was lowering my omelette between us... (*She bursts out laughing and slaps her thigh. He sees this and his smile remains. The tea kettle whistles behind the counter.*)

PROPRIETRESS. Milk or lemon? (*He watches her a moment, smiling.*) Lemon?

MAN. Lemon, yes. (*She goes and pours tea. Man, with a new anticipatory excitement.*) You're not busy?

PROPRIETRESS. After Christmas it all dies for a few days. (*Hands him a cup.*)

MAN. It's more like somebody's home in here.

PROPRIETRESS. I try to sell only what I'd conceivably want for myself, yes.

MAN. You're successful.

PROPRIETRESS. In a way. (*Confusing.*) ... I am, I guess.—Very, in fact.

MAN. But a baby would be better.

PROPRIETRESS. (*A flash of resentment, but then truth.*) ... Sometimes. (*Hesitates.*) Often, actually. (*Looks around at the shop.*) It's all simply numbers, figures. Something appalling about business, something totally pointless—like emptying a pail and filling it again every day.—Why?—Do I look unhappy?

MAN. You look like you'd found yourself... for the fiftieth time

13

and would love to throw yourself away again.

PROPRIETRESS. You try to avoid hurting people.

MAN. Yes, but it can't be helped sometimes. I've done it.

PROPRIETRESS. No wonder she loves you.

MAN. I'm not so sure. I really don't know anymore.

PROPRIETRESS. Oh, it must be true.

MAN. Why?

PROPRIETRESS. It would be so easy.

MAN. But I'm so old.

PROPRIETRESS. No.

MAN. I'm not sure I want her to. I warned her not to, soon after we started. I said there was no future in it. I said that these things are usually a case of loving yourself and wanting someone else to confirm it, that's all. I said all the blunt and ugly things I could think of.

PROPRIETRESS. And it didn't matter at all. (*Slight pause.*)

MAN. It didn't?

PROPRIETRESS. (*With a hard truthfulness.*) Of course it mattered—what you said made her stamp on her feelings, and hold part of herself in reserve. It even humiliated her a little.

MAN. (*In defense.*) But her independence means more to her than any relationship, I think.

PROPRIETRESS. How do you know?—You were the one who ordered her not to love you . . .

MAN. Yes. (*Evading her eyes.*) But there's no tragic error, necessarily—I don't think she wanted to love anyone. In fact, I don't think either of us said or did anything we badly regret— it's Nature that made the mistake; that I should be so much older, and so perfectly healthy and she so young and sick.

PROPRIETRESS. (*Unnerved, an outburst.*) Why do you go on assuming it has to be the end! (*He looks at her with surprise.*) Thousands of people survive these things. And why couldn't you ask her what exactly it was?

MAN. I couldn't bear to make her say it.

PROPRIETRESS. Then all she's actually said was that an operation . . ?

MAN. No. Just that the 28th of the month was the big day.

PROPRIETRESS. (*Almost victoriously.*) Well that could mean

almost anything.

MAN. (*In anguish.*) Then why doesn't she let me come and see her!

PROPRIETRESS. (*Frantically.*) Because she doesn't want to load her troubles onto you!

MAN. I've thought of that.

PROPRIETRESS. Of course. It's a matter of pride. Even before this happened, I'm sure she never encouraged you to just drop in, for instance—did she?

MAN. Oh no. On the contrary.

PROPRIETRESS. Of course not! She wanted her hair to be done and be dressed in something you'd like her in ...

MAN. Oh, insisted on that, yes.

PROPRIETRESS. Then you can hardly expect her to invite you to see her in a hospital! (*Slight pause.*)

MAN. Then it *is* all pretty superficial, isn't it.

PROPRIETRESS. Why!—it could be the most important thing in her entire life.

MAN. (*Pause. Shakes his head.*) No. Important—but not the most important. Because neither of us have burned our bridges. As how could we?—If only because of my age?

PROPRIETRESS. Why do you go on about your age? That's only an excuse to escape with.

MAN. (*Smiles.*) But it's the only one I've got, dear.—But whatever age I was, she wouldn't be good to be married to.

PROPRIETRESS. (*Hurt, almost alarmed.*) How can you say that!

MAN. What's wrong in saying it? She's still ambitious for herself, she still needs risks, accomplishments, new expectations; she needs the dangerous mountains not marriage in the valley—marriage would leave her restless, it would never last. (*Pause.*)

PROPRIETRESS. (*Dryly.*) Well, then ... you were both satisfied ... (*As he turns to her, surprised.*) ... with what you had.

MAN. That's a surprise—I never thought of that. Yes; very nearly. (*Thinks further.*) Almost. Yes. (*Slight pause.*) That's a shock, now.

PROPRIETRESS. To realize that you were almost perfectly happy.

MAN. Almost—You see, there was always—of necessity—some-

15

thing so tentative about it and uncertain, that I never thought of it as perfect, but it was—a perfect chaos. Amazing.

PROPRIETRESS. And your wife?

MAN. (*Slight pause.*) My wife is who I should be married to. We've always helped one another. I'll always be grateful for having her. Especially her kindness.

PROPRIETRESS. She's not ambitious.

MAN. Yes; within bounds. We're partners in a business—advisory service for town planners. She's tremendously competent; I oversee; do less and less, though.

PROPRIETRESS. Why? Isn't it important?

MAN. Certainly is—we've changed whole countrysides for the next hundred years.

PROPRIETRESS. Then why do less and less?

MAN. I won't be here in a hundred years.—That struck me powerfully one morning. (*Pause.*)

PROPRIETRESS. So—all in all—you will survive this.

MAN. (*Catching the implied rebuke.*) That's right. And in a while, whole days will go by when her anguish barely crosses my mind; and then weeks, and then months, I imagine. (*Slight pause.*) And as I say this, I know that at this very moment she may well be keeping herself hidden from me so as not to wound me with her dying.

PROPRIETRESS. Or wound herself. (*He looks at her questioningly.*) If she doesn't have to look at what she's lost she loses less.—But I don't believe it's as bad as you make it. She's only keeping you away so that you won't see her so frightened of the knife. She has sense.

MAN. But why!—I would try to comfort her!

PROPRIETRESS. (*Strongly, angrily protesting.*) But she doesn't want comfort, she wants her power back! You came to her for happiness, not some torn flesh bleeding on the sheets! She knows how long pity lasts! (*Slight pause.*)

MAN. Then what are you saying?—That there is really no gift I can give her at all?—Is that what you say? (*Proprietress, silent, lowers her eyes.*) There is really nothing between us, is there—nothing but an...uncommitment? (*Grins.*) Maybe that's why it's so hard to think of something to give her...She

16

asked me once—as we were getting up at the end of an evening—she said, "Can you remember all the women you've had?" Because she couldn't remember all her men, she said.

PROPRIETRESS. And did you believe her?

MAN. No. I thought she was merely reassuring me of her indifference—that she'd never become demanding. It chilled me up the spine.

PROPRIETRESS. Really! Why?

MAN. Why say such a thing unless she had a terrific urge to hold onto me?

PROPRIETRESS. But now you've changed your mind... (*He turns to her surprised.*)

MAN. No, I kind of think now she was telling the truth. I think there is some flow of indifference in her, cold and remote, like water flowing in a cave. As there is in me. (*Slight pause.*) I feel you're condemning me now.

PROPRIETRESS. I never condemn anyone; you know that. I can't.

MAN. I know. But still, deep, deep down....

PROPRIETRESS. No. I'm helpless not to forgive everything, finally.

MAN. That's your glory, but in some deepest part of you there has to be some touch of comtempt...

PROPRIETRESS. What are you saying?—You carefully offered only your friendship, didn't you?

MAN. But what more could I offer!

PROPRIETRESS. Then you can't expect what you would have had if you'd committed yourself, can you.

MAN. What I would have had..?

PROPRIETRESS. Yes!—To be clung to now, to be worn out with weeping, to be staggered with your new loneliness, to be clarified with grief, washed with it, cleansed by a whole sorrow. A lover has to earn that satisfaction. If you couldn't bring yourself to share her life, you can't expect to share her dying. Is that what you'd like?

MAN. I would like to understand what I was to her.

PROPRIETRESS. (*Protesting.*) You were her friend!

MAN. (*Shakes his head.*) There is no such thing. No! No! No!

What is a friend who only wants the good news and the bright side? I love her. But I am forbidden to by my commitments, by my age, by my aching joints—great God almighty, I'm sleepy by half-past nine! The whole thing is ludicrous, what could she have seen in me? I can't bear the sight of my face in the mirror—I'm shaving my father every morning!

PROPRIETRESS. Then why not believe her—you were ... simply one of her friends.

MAN. (*Pause.*) One of her ... friends. Yes.—I'll have to try to accept that. (*Slight pause.*) But why doesn't it empty me? Why am I still filled like this? What should I do that I haven't done—or say that I haven't said to make some breakthrough? (*Weeping.*) My God, what am I saying! (*Imploring.*) You know. Tell me!

PROPRIETRESS. Perhaps ... that it's perfect, just as it is? (*He slowly turns from her, absorbing her voice.*) That it is all that it could ever have become? (*Pause.*)

MAN. You feel that?—You believe that?

PROPRIETRESS. Yes.

MAN. ... That we are as close now as we can ever come?

PROPRIETRESS. Yes.—But she believes she's going to make it, she knows she'll live.

MAN. So she's simply ... momentarily afraid.

PROPRIETRESS. Oh, terribly, yes.

MAN. (*With gathering hope.*) That's possible; and it's true that she'd never wish to be seen that scared, especially by me. She has contempt for cowardice, she rises to any show of bravery— any! I think you're possibly right; she'll want to see me when she's made it! When she's a winner again!

PROPRIETRESS. I'm sure of it.

MAN. On the other hand ... (*Breaks off suddenly; as though a hollowness opens beneath him his face goes expressionless.*) ... it's also possible, isn't it ... that ...

PROPRIETRESS. (*Cutting him off, with dread.*) Why go further? You'll know everything soon.

MAN. Not if I can't see her. She won't say the name of the hospital.

18

PROPRIETRESS. (*She touches his hand.*) But why go further?

MAN. But if she...dies?

PROPRIETRESS. She doesn't expect to.

MAN. (*With confidence, an awareness.*) Or she does expect to. (*And he turns to her; she is filled with love and anguish; he speaks directly to her, gripping her hand in his.*) Either way, my being with her now...would only deepen it between us when it should not be deepened, because very soon now I will be far too old. If she makes it...it would not be good for us—to have shared such agony. It won't cure age, nothing will—*That's* it. (*She offers her lips, he kisses her.*)It's that she doesn't want it spoiled you see, by deepening.

PROPRIETRESS. (*She embraces him, her body pressed to his, an immense longing in it and a sense of a last embrace.*) She wants to make it stay exactly as it is...forever. (*She presses his face to hers, they kiss.*) How gently! (*He kisses her again. With a near cry of farewell...*) Oh how gently! (*He slips from her embrace; a new thought as he looks around the shop.*)

MAN. Then what I ought to send her is something she could definitely keep for a long time. (*He is quickened as he looks about, as though he almost knows beforehand what to seek. He moves more quickly from object to object, and at a tray of costume jewelry he halts, draws out a watch on a gold chain.*) Does this work? (*Winds it.*)

PROPRIETRESS. Oh yes, it's exact. It's an antique.

MAN. (*Puts the watch to his ear, then couches it in his hand, hefts it, then hangs it from the neck of the Proprietress and stands back to look at it on her.*) Yes, it's beautiful.

PROPRIETRESS. I know. (*He starts to take out his wallet...*) Take it. (*She takes it off her neck and holds it out, hanging it before him; he puts back his wallet. The implication freezes him.*) Go ahead—it's just the right thing; it will tell her to be brave each time she looks at it. (*He takes the watch and chain and looks at them in his hand.*) You never said her name. (*She starts to smile.*)

MAN. (*Starting to smile.*) You never said yours. (*Slight pause.*) Thank you. Thank you...very much. (*On each of their faces a grin spreads—of deep familiarity. The light begins to lower; with the smile still on his face he moves away from the setting until he is facing front, staring. The woman and the boutique go dark, vanishing. He strolls away, alone.)*

The End

PROPERTY LIST

Assorted boutique items:
  Gloves
  Blouses
  Silk kerchiefs
  Negligees
  Sweaters
Bust with sweater draped over it
Bust with necklace
Upturned plastic thigh with garter
Arm with wristwatch
Plastic head with knitted cap & muffler
Counter
Display case, on counter, with jewelry
Tea kettle, behind counter
Tea cups
Milk & lemon, for tea
Tray of costume jewelry with watch on gold chain
Wallet (Man)

NEW PLAYS

★ **HONOUR by Joanna Murray-Smith.** In a series of intense confrontations, a wife, husband, lover and daughter negotiate the forces of passion, history, responsibility and honour. "HONOUR makes for surprisingly interesting viewing. Tight, crackling dialogue (usually played out in punchy verbal duels) captures characters unable to deal with emotions ... Murray-Smith effectively places her characters in situations that strip away pretense." –*Variety* "... the play's virtues are strong: a distinctive theatrical voice, passionate concerns ... HONOUR might just capture a few honors of its own." –*Time Out Magazine* [1M, 3W] ISBN: 0-8222-1683-3

★ **MR. PETERS' CONNECTIONS by Arthur Miller.** Mr. Miller describes the protagonist as existing in a dream-like state when the mind is "freed to roam from real memories to conjectures, from trivialities to tragic insights, from terror of death to glorying in one's being alive." With this memory play, the Tony Award and Pulitzer Prize-winner reaffirms his stature as the world's foremost dramatist. "... a cross between Joycean stream-of-consciousness and Strindberg's dream plays, sweetened with a dose of William Saroyan's philosophical whimsy ... CONNECTIONS is most intriguing ..." –*The NY Times* [5M, 3W] ISBN: 0-8222-1687-6

★ **THE WAITING ROOM by Lisa Loomer.** Three women from different centuries meet in a doctor's waiting room in this dark comedy about the timeless quest for beauty – and its cost. "... THE WAITING ROOM ... is a bold, risky melange of conflicting elements that is ... terrifically moving ... There's no resisting the fierce emotional pull of the play." –*The NY Times* "... one of the high points of this year's Off-Broadway season ... THE WAITING ROOM is well worth a visit." –*Back Stage* [7M, 4W, flexible casting] ISBN: 0-8222-1594-2

★ **THE OLD SETTLER by John Henry Redwood.** A sweet-natured comedy about two church-going sisters in 1943 Harlem and the handsome young man who rents a room in their apartment. "For all of its decent sentiments, THE OLD SETTLER avoids sentimentality. It has the authenticity and lack of pretense of an Early American sampler." –*The NY Times* "We've had some fine plays Off-Broadway this season, and this is one of the best." –*The NY Post* [1M, 3W] ISBN: 0-8-222-1642-6

★ **LAST TRAIN TO NIBROC by Arlene Hutton.** In 1940 two young strangers share a seat on a train bound east only to find their paths will cross again. "All aboard. LAST TRAIN TO NIBROC is a sweetly told little chamber romance." –*Show Business* "... [a] gently charming little play, reminiscent of Thornton Wilder in its look at rustic Americans who are to be treasured for their simplicity and directness ..." –*Associated Press* "The old formula of boy wins girl, boy loses girl, boy wins girl still works ... [a] well-made play that perfectly captures a slice of small-town-life-gone-by." –*Back Stage* [1M, 1W] ISBN: 0-8222-1753-8

★ **OVER THE RIVER AND THROUGH THE WOODS by Joe DiPietro.** Nick sees both sets of his grandparents every Sunday for dinner. This is routine until he has to tell them that he's been offered a dream job in Seattle. The news doesn't sit so well. "A hilarious family comedy that is even funnier than his long running musical revue *I Love You, You're Perfect, Now Change*." –*Back Stage* "Loaded with laughs every step of the way." –*Star-Ledger* [3M, 3W] ISBN: 0-8222-1712-0

★ **SIDE MAN by Warren Leight.** 1999 Tony Award winner. This is the story of a broken family and the decline of jazz as popular entertainment. "... a tender, deeply personal memory play about the turmoil in the family of a jazz musician as his career crumbles at the dawn of the age of rock-and-roll ..." –*The NY Times* "[SIDE MAN] is an elegy for two things – a lost world and a lost love. When the two notes sound together in harmony, it is moving and graceful ..." –*The NY Daily News* "An atmospheric memory play ... with crisp dialogue and clearly drawn characters ... reflects the passing of an era with persuasive insight ... The joy and despair of the musicians is skillfully illustrated." –*Variety* [5M, 3W] ISBN: 0-8222-1721-X

DRAMATISTS PLAY SERVICE, INC.
440 Park Avenue South, New York, NY 10016 212-683-8960 Fax 212-213-1539
postmaster@dramatists.com www.dramatists.com

NEW PLAYS

★ **CLOSER by Patrick Marber.** Winner of the 1998 Olivier Award for Best Play and the 1999 New York Drama Critics Circle Award for Best Foreign Play. Four lives intertwine over the course of four and a half years in this densely plotted, stinging look at modern love and betrayal. "CLOSER is a sad, savvy, often funny play that casts a steely, unblinking gaze at the world of relationships and lets you come to your own conclusions ... CLOSER does not merely hold your attention; it burrows into you." –*New York Magazine* "A powerful, darkly funny play about the cosmic collision between the sun of love and the comet of desire." –*Newsweek Magazine* [2M, 2W] ISBN: 0-8222-1722-8

★ **THE MOST FABULOUS STORY EVER TOLD by Paul Rudnick.** A stage manager, headset and prompt book at hand, brings the house lights to half, then dark, and cues the creation of the world. Throughout the play, she's in control of everything. In other words, she's either God, or she thinks she is. "Line by line, Mr. Rudnick may be the funniest writer for the stage in the United States today ... One-liners, epigrams, withering put-downs and flashing repartee: These are the candles that Mr. Rudnick lights instead of cursing the darkness ... a testament to the virtues of laughing ... and in laughter, there is something like the memory of Eden." –*The NY Times* "Funny it is ... consistently, rapaciously, deliriously ... easily the funniest play in town." –*Variety* [4M, 5W] ISBN: 0-8222-1720-1

★ **A DOLL'S HOUSE by Henrik Ibsen, adapted by Frank McGuinness.** Winner of the 1997 Tony Award for Best Revival. "New, raw, gut-twisting and gripping. Easily the hottest drama this season." –*USA Today* "Bold, brilliant and alive." –*The Wall Street Journal* "A thunderclap of an evening that takes your breath away." –*Time Magazine* [4M, 4W, 2 boys] ISBN: 0-8222-1636-1

★ **THE HERBAL BED by Peter Whelan.** The play is based on actual events which occurred in Stratford-upon-Avon in the summer of 1613, when William Shakespeare's elder daughter was publicly accused of having a sexual liaison with a married neighbor and family friend. "In his probing new play, THE HERBAL BED ... Peter Whelan muses about a sidelong event in the life of Shakespeare's family and creates a finely textured tapestry of love and lies in the early 17th-century Stratford." –*The NY Times* "It is a first rate drama with interesting moral issues of truth and expediency." –*The NY Post* [5M, 3W] ISBN: 0-8222-1675-2

★ **SNAKEBIT by David Marshall Grant.** A study of modern friendship when put to the test. "... a rather smart and absorbing evening of water-cooler theater, the intimate sort of Off-Broadway experience that has you picking apart the recognizable characters long after the curtain calls." – *The NY Times* "Off-Broadway keeps on presenting us with compelling reasons for going to the theater. The latest is SNAKEBIT, David Marshall Grant's smart new comic drama about being thirtysomething and losing one's way in life." –*The NY Daily News* [3M, 1W] ISBN: 0-8222-1724-4

★ **A QUESTION OF MERCY by David Rabe.** The Obie Award-winning playwright probes the sensitive and controversial issue of doctor-assisted suicide in the age of AIDS in this poignant drama. "There are many devastating ironies in Mr. Rabe's beautifully considered, piercingly clear-eyed work ..." –*The NY Times* "With unsettling candor and disturbing insight, the play arouses pity and understanding of a troubling subject ... Rabe's provocative tale is an affirmation of dignity that rings clear and true." –*Variety* [6M, 1W] ISBN: 0-8222-1643-4

★ **DIMLY PERCEIVED THREATS TO THE SYSTEM by Jon Klein.** Reality and fantasy overlap with hilarious results as this unforgettable family attempts to survive the nineties. "Here's a play whose point about fractured families goes to the heart, mind – and ears." –*The Washington Post* "... an end-of-the-millennium comedy about a family on the verge of a nervous breakdown ... Trenchant and hilarious ..." –*The Baltimore Sun* [2M, 4W] ISBN: 0-8222-1677-9

DRAMATISTS PLAY SERVICE, INC.
440 Park Avenue South, New York, NY 10016 212-683-8960 Fax 212-213-1539
postmaster@dramatists.com www.dramatists.com

NEW PLAYS

★ **AS BEES IN HONEY DROWN by Douglas Carter Beane.** Winner of the John Gassner Playwriting Award. A hot young novelist finds the subject of his new screenplay in a New York socialite who leads him into the world of *Auntie Mame* and *Breakfast at Tiffany's,* before she takes him for a ride. "A delicious soufflé of a satire ... [an] extremely entertaining fable for an age that always chooses image over substance." *–The NY Times* "... A witty assessment of one of the most active and relentless industries in a consumer society ... the creation of 'hot' young things, which the media have learned to mass produce with efficiency and zeal." *–The NY Daily News* [3M, 3W, flexible casting] ISBN: 0-8222-1651-5

★ **STUPID KIDS by John C. Russell.** In rapid, highly stylized scenes, the story follows four high-school students as they make their way from first through eighth period and beyond, struggling with the fears, frustrations, and longings peculiar to youth. "In STUPID KIDS ... playwright John C. Russell gets the opera of adolescence to a T ... The stylized teenspeak of STUPID KIDS ... suggests that Mr. Russell may have hidden a tape recorder under a desk in study hall somewhere and then scoured the tapes for good quotations ... it is the kids' insular, ceaselessly churning world, a pre-adult world of Doritos and libidos, that the playwright seeks to lay bare." *–The NY Times* "STUPID KIDS [is] a sharp-edged ... whoosh of teen angst and conformity anguish. It is also very funny." *–NY Newsday* [2M, 2W] ISBN: 0-8222-1698-1

★ **COLLECTED STORIES by Donald Margulies.** From Obie Award-winner Donald Margulies comes a provocative analysis of a student-teacher relationship that turns sour when the protégé becomes a rival. "With his fine ear for detail, Margulies creates an authentic, insular world, and he gives equal weight to the opposing viewpoints of two formidable characters." *–The LA Times* "This is probably Margulies' best play to date ..." *–The NY Post* "... always fluid and lively, the play is thick with ideas, like a stock-pot of good stew." *–The Village Voice* [2W] ISBN: 0-8222-1640-X

★ **FREEDOMLAND by Amy Freed.** An overdue showdown between a son and his father sets off fireworks that illuminate the neurosis, rage and anxiety of one family – and of America at the turn of the millennium. "FREEDOMLAND's more obvious links are to *Buried Child* and *Bosoms and Neglect.* Freed, like Guare, is an inspired wordsmith with a gift for surreal touches in situations grounded in familiar and real territory." *–Curtain Up* [3M, 4W] ISBN: 0-8222-1719-8

★ **STOP KISS by Diana Son.** A poignant and funny play about the ways, both sudden and slow, that lives can change irrevocably. "There's so much that is vital and exciting about STOP KISS ... you want to embrace this young author and cheer her onto other works ... the writing on display here is funny and credible ... you also will be charmed by its heartfelt characters and up-to-the-minute humor." *–The NY Daily News* "... irresistibly exciting ... a sweet, sad, and enchantingly sincere play." *–The NY Times* [3M, 3W] ISBN: 0-8222-1731-7

★ **THREE DAYS OF RAIN by Richard Greenberg.** The sins of fathers and mothers make for a bittersweet elegy in this poignant and revealing drama. "... a work so perfectly judged it heralds the arrival of a major playwright ... Greenberg is extraordinary." *–The NY Daily News* "Greenberg's play is filled with graceful passages that are by turns melancholy, harrowing, and often, quite funny." *–Variety* [2M, 1W] ISBN: 0-8222-1676-0

★ **THE WEIR by Conor McPherson.** In a bar in rural Ireland, the local men swap spooky stories in an attempt to impress a young woman from Dublin who recently moved into a nearby "haunted" house. However, the tables are soon turned when she spins a yarn of her own. "You shed all sense of time at this beautiful and devious new play." *–The NY Times* "Sheer theatrical magic. I have rarely been so convinced that I have just seen a modern classic. Tremendous." *–The London Daily Telegraph* [4M, 1W] ISBN: 0-8222-1706-6

DRAMATISTS PLAY SERVICE, INC.
440 Park Avenue South, New York, NY 10016 212-683-8960 Fax 212-213-1539
postmaster@dramatists.com www.dramatists.com